Mussolini

Sandra Woodcock

Published in association with The Basic Skills Agency

Hodder & Stoughton
A MEMBER OF THE HODDER HEADLINE GROUP

Acknowledgements

Photos: p. 4 © Popperfoto, pp. 8, 11, 19 © Hulton Deutsch, pp. 14, 17 © Camera Press, p. 22 © Keystone, p. 25 © Corbis-Bettmann.

Cover photo: © Popperfoto/Reuter.

Orders: please contact Bookpoint Ltd, 39 Milton Park, Abingdon, Oxon OX14 4TD. Telephone: (44) 01235 400414, Fax: (44) 01235 400454. Lines are open from 9.00–6.00, Monday to Saturday, with a 24 hour message answering service. Email address: orders@bookpoint.co.uk

British Library Cataloguing in Publication Data
A catalogue record for this title is available from The British Library

ISBN 0 340 71163 9

First published 1998
Impression number 10 9 8 7 6 5 4 3 2 1
Year 2003 2002 2001 2000 1999 1998

Typeset by Fakenham Photosetting Ltd, Fakenham, Norfolk.
Printed in Great Britain for Hodder & Stoughton Educational, a division of Hodder Headline Plc, 338 Euston Road, London NW1 3BH by Page Bros Ltd, Norwich.

Contents

Benito Mussolini was the son of a blacksmith.
His family was poor and he was a nobody.
Yet by the age of 29
everyone in Italy knew his name.
He was the leader of the Italian people.

Mussolini had great power in Italy
because the people loved him.
But he was a brutal man.
He took his people on a path to war and disaster.
In the end he was hated and killed
by his own people.
His dead body was kicked and trampled on
by an angry mob.

This is the story of his life.

1 A Wild Child

Mussolini was born in 1883.
He grew up in a small village
in the north of Italy.
His family was poor, but so were
most of their friends and neighbours.
It was quite common for
a boy and his father to share
one pair of shoes.
They were always short of food or fuel.
People would say:
'If you want to get warm, skip.'

When he was a little boy,
Mussolini was a wild child.
He did not talk much,
but was good at using his fists.
At the age of eight, he was running wild.
He was always stealing
and getting into fights.
His father told him
he must stick up for himself.

At school,
Mussolini was always in trouble.
He was expelled for
stabbing a boy in his bottom.

In his teens he was good-looking,
with large dark eyes.
He had many affairs with many women,
but he had no real respect for women.

He was wild
but he was also keen to get on in life.
He wanted to be important.
He wanted to make his mark in a big way.

Mussolini spent a lot of time reading.
He would read about politics and power.

He left home to be a teacher.
He moved to a town 100 miles away.
Then he went to Switzerland.

Benito Mussolini.

When he came back to his home,
he met a waitress called Rachel.

He was no romantic hero.
He walked into her sister's house and said:
'I want Rachel to be
the mother of my children.
But tell her to hurry, I'm pushed for time.'

Rachel did not even have time to comb her hair.
She walked in the rain to her new home.
They had very little money.

Soon Rachel had a baby girl.
It was five years before
Mussolini and Rachel married.
In that time she had a second baby.
Mussolini was also seeing other women.
He had a son by one of them.

Mussolini had started up a small newspaper.
Most of the work was done from his home.
Soon, he moved on to work for
a bigger newspaper.
He was angry about the way poor people lived.
He wanted change
and he thought violence was the way to get it.
The newspaper put over his ideas.

2 Hard Times

In 1914 World War One began.
Italians had to go and fight.
Mussolini spent two years in the army.

After the war
there was a lot of trouble in Italy.
Soldiers who came home could not find jobs.
Prices were high,
so poor people could not afford to buy food.

There were strikes in towns.
There was trouble on the streets.
Gangs of poor people set fire to
the houses of the rich farmers.
Everyone was afraid of something.

The government did not help them.
Mussolini could feel the mood
of the people.
He could see the anger of the ex-soldiers.
He called a meeting
and started a new political party.
He called it the Fascist Party.

Mussolini in army uniform.

But they did not act like a political party.
The Fascists were men of violence.
They wore black shirts.
They were thugs and bullies
looking for a fight.

Mussolini told them
to deal with Italy's problems.
They would make Italy a strong country.

When there were strikes,
the Fascists came and beat up the strikers.
Rich men called on the Fascists to help them.
The government
could not deal with troublemakers.
The Fascists could.

The Fascists had battles on the streets
with Communists.
They beat up the Communists
and made them drink bottles of castor oil.

People in Italy said they needed
a strong leader.
They wanted Mussolini
to lead the country.
More people voted for the Fascists.

In the summer of 1922
there was a big strike in Italy.
There were no buses or trains.
Again, the police and the government
did nothing.
The Fascists ended the strike.
They got the trains running again.

Mussolini said
it was a good time to take power.
In October he planned a march
into the city of Rome.
He said:
'The government will be given to us
or we shall take it.'

Mussolini giving a speech.

Thousands of men
in black shirts came together.
They were ready
to march into Rome.

What would the King do?
He could have ordered the army
to stop the Fascists.
The army could have stopped them.
But the King did not give the order.
He asked Mussolini
to be the Prime Minister.

3 The Leader

Now Mussolini began
to make changes in Italy.
There would be no other political parties.
The people could vote only for the Fascists.
Children and young people
had to learn Fascist ideas.
They had to learn to be strong.

Mussolini said:
'To live one day as a lion
is better than 100 years as a sheep.'

Children had to join Fascist youth groups.
They trained to be soldiers.
They learned these words:
Believe, Obey, Fight.

People did speak out against the Fascists.
But they were treated very badly.
They were put in prison or even killed.

14

Mussolini was made out to be a strong man.
People thought he could do anything.
A light was left on in his office all night,
so people would think that he was working.
But it was a trick.

Mussolini was like a showman.
He was good at speaking to crowds.
The people loved to see him
and he knew how to make them happy.
They would cheer every word.
'A crowd is like a woman,' he said,
'a crowd likes a strong man.'

The people of Italy
saw pictures of Mussolini everywhere.
There were pictures of him riding horses,
boxing and doing other sports.
But he was not as fit as he made out.
He ate too much. He had an ulcer
and had to be put on a diet.

The people were told what a good husband
and father he was.
He told Italian mothers
to have many children.
But he hardly saw his family.
He lived in hotels and had many other women.

It was at this time,
when he was 50,
that he began his affair with Clara.
She was a woman half his age.

Mussolini lied to the Italian people
about most things.
He told the world
that Italy was great and strong.
He boasted about the big navy.
He boasted about the air force.
It was not true. When war came,
the people of Italy would see their leader
for what he was: a con man.

Mussolini with Hitler.

4 War

Mussolini wanted Italy to be a world power.
He was willing to fight wars to win glory.
He won a war in North Africa.

He made friends
with the German leader Adolf Hitler.
Hitler was a fan of Mussolini.
He wrote and asked for a photo of him.
Mussolini laughed at Hitler
when he first met him.
He called him a clown.

But Hitler soon became powerful
and Mussolini wanted him as a friend.
Italy and Germany made a treaty in 1939.
It was called the 'Pact of Steel'.
Mussolini had promised to
support Hitler in war.

Italy was not ready for war.
Mussolini needed four years to be ready.
But in just a few months
World War Two began.
Hitler called on him to go to war.

Mussolini with his troops.

Mussolini was not worried.
He said the war would be over
in a few months.
He thought Hitler would win.
But he was wrong.

As Hitler took over Europe,
Mussolini joined in.
But war led to shame for Italy.
The Italian army tried three times
to take over Greece.
They could not do it.
The Germans had to help them.

In North Africa,
the Italians were no match for the British.
Thousands of Italians were taken prisoner.

At last Mussolini had to put his armies
under German control.

Hitler's wars were bad for Italy.
But Mussolini still followed
everything Hitler did.
Even when Hitler invaded Russia,
Italian soldiers were sent.
Soon Italy was at war with the USA.

It was madness.
By 1942, Italy was pushed to the limit.
Their armies were beaten everywhere.
They were hungry.
They were short of weapons.
At home in Italy,
the people were short of food.

People were angry
and turned against the war.
They saw that Mussolini had lied.
Now their own country was invaded
by British and American armies.

Mussolini was the most hated man in Italy.
The King had him arrested.

His 'prison' was a ski hotel
high in the mountains.
The great Mussolini was now a sad, old man.

But Hitler had not forgotten his friend.
He sent a team of SS men to find Mussolini.
At last they found out where he was.
A rescue plane took Mussolini to Germany.
Hitler told him he must not give up.
He had to go back to Italy.
He must try to keep the Fascists in power.

5 A Nasty End

Mussolini did go back to Italy.
He was there for the last year of the war.
It was a mistake.
The war could not be won.
In the end the Fascists were hunted
by their own people.
Mussolini tried to leave Italy
with his mistress Clara.
They took a lift in a car going to the border.
But the driver stopped the car.
He told them to get out.
He took out a gun
and said he had orders to shoot them.
He did it in the name of the people of Italy.

More Fascists were shot in a village near by.
All the bodies were put in a furniture van
and driven to the city of Milan.

The bodies of Mussolini and Clara
were hung upside down
outside a petrol station.
People came to shout insults,
to spit at them and to throw things.
The mob lost control.
They kicked and shot at the dead bodies.
All their hatred was coming out.

Mussolini had been like a god
to the people of Italy.
Now they wanted to kill him
over and over again.
When it was all over,
his body was taken away.
He had to be buried secretly in Milan.

In 1957 the body was given to his family
to be buried near to his home town.